Religion verses Homosexuality

Rev. James R. D. Yeaw, D.Div.

Unity Spiritual Center

First Edition, 2017
Library of Congress Cataloging-in-Publication Data
Yeaw, James R. D.
Religion verses Homosexuality / James Yeaw
 P. cm
Includes index

ISBN-13: 978-1979561426
ISBN-10: 1979561427

1. Homosexuality   3. Christian Theology

Table of Contents

Questions About Homosexuality

This material is presented because of questions that have arisen in the media and in our own community over the past weeks. We are presenting these essays and our conclusions. First, one from David Lose of the *Huffington Post*.

What Does Judeo-Christian Writings Really Say About Homosexuality?

A whole lot less than you might imagine! That may be hard to believe given the fierce rhetoric Christians often employ when talking about homosexuality, but there are only seven passages in the Bible that refer directly to homosexual behavior, and none of them are associated with Jesus. Compare that to the more than 250 verses on the proper use of wealth or more than 300 on our responsibility to care for the poor and work for justice, and you appreciate quickly that homosexuality was not exactly a major theme of the Bible.

Nevertheless, these seven passages have been poured over by conservative and liberal scholars alike and have occasioned considerable conversation and controversy. To review what the Bible says about homosexuality, as well as what others are saying about it, I'll group similar verses below and give a summary of the major differences in interpretation. Then, I'll outline the four most common stances Christians take regarding these biblical passages in general, as these positions greatly influence how one interprets individual verses.[1]

---

[1] *Note: For a more detailed treatment of these passages, see Background Essay on Biblical Texts for "Journey Together Faithfully, Part Two: The Church and Homosexuality" by Arland J. Hultgren and Walter F. Taylor Jr., two well respected biblical scholars who disagree on the issues at hand. I have at several points been guided by their work.*

What is the Hebrew Scripture Narrative?

There are two passages that refer to homosexual behavior that are set in larger narratives. That is, they are part of a story, not a legal or moral code. Each deal with the threat of homosexual rape. The more famous of the two comes from the story of Sodom and Gomorrah found in Genesis.[2] Lot, Abraham's nephew, is staying in Sodom when he is visited by angels. Men from the city come and demand that they be allowed to have sex with Lot's guests. Lot refuses and when he is threatened by the townspeople the angels he has hosted protect him. A similar story occurs in Judges[3] minus angels and with a grislier outcome.

There is broad consensus among scholars on both the left and the right that these passages have nothing to do with homosexuality per se, but rather with hospitality and justice. That is, both scenes represent hosts protecting their guests from severe humiliation and outrageous injustice. Some other parts of the Bible interpret these passages just this way. Ezekiel, for instance, refers to the sin of Sodom not in terms of sexual immorality but rather justice:

This was the guilt of your sister Sodom: she and her daughters had pride, excess of food, and prosperous ease, but did not aid the poor and needy.[4]

What is the Holiness Code of Leviticus?

There are two verses in the book of Leviticus that refer to homosexual behavior. The first reads, "You shall not lie with a male as with a woman; it is an abomination".[5] While the second goes even further: "If a man lies with a male as with a woman, both of them have committed an abomination; they shall be put to death; their blood is upon them".[6] Again, there is considerable agreement that both of these passages are portions of what is commonly called the holiness code, a set of rules and regulations

---

2 Genesis 19:1-11
3 Judges 19:16-30
4 Ezekiel 16:49
5 Leviticus 18:22
6 Leviticus 20:13

spanning chapters 17-26 that are intended to set Israel apart from the Egyptians they fled and the Canaanites they were now living among.

There is considerable debate, however, about three matters:

1. Do these passages refer to consensual homosexual practice (and whether that was even a recognized option in the ancient world), or do they describe the cultic practice of Israel's neighbors and adversaries?
2. Are these regulations contingent because they derive from particular challenges and situations the Israelites faced at that time (the importance of procreation, for instance, given that Israel was a nomadic people dependent on increasing its population for survival), or do they intend to establish universal sexual norms?
3. And even if these regulations were normative for Israelites, do they continue to be for Christians given how many other Levitical codes are contradicted later in the New Testament or have historically been ignored by Christians.[7]

What about Christian ethical teachings?

The three passages in question read as follows:

Romans 1:26-27: "For this reason God gave them up to degrading passions. Their women exchanged natural intercourse for unnatural, and in the same way also the men, giving up natural intercourse with women, were consumed with passion for one another. Men committed shameless acts with men and received in their own persons the due penalty for their error."

1 Corinthians 6:9-11: "Do you not know that wrongdoers will not inherit the kingdom of God? Do not be deceived!

---

[7] Examples: Stoning children who disobey; Abominations include eating of shellfish, wearing mixed fibers, planting two different crops in the same field, or failing to build a parapet around the roof of one's house.

Fornicators, idolaters, adulterers, male prostitutes, sodomites, thieves, the greedy, drunkards, revilers, robbers — none of these will inherit the kingdom of God. And this is what some of you used to be. But you were washed, you were sanctified, you were justified in the name of the Lord Jesus Christ and in the Spirit of our God."

I Timothy 1:9-11: "This means understanding that the law is laid down not for the innocent but for the lawless and disobedient, for the godless and sinful, for the unholy and profane, for those who kill their father or mother, for murderers, fornicators, sodomites, slave-traders, liars, perjurers, and whatever else is contrary to the sound teaching that conforms to the glorious gospel of the blessed God, which he entrusted to me."

There is considerable debate on at least two questions about these passages:

1. Do they refer to consensual homosexual practice, to cultic prostitution or to male pederasty (where an adult male has sex with a younger boy, either as a coming of age ritual or on a commercial basis)?

2. Are the authors pointing to specific behavior they have witnessed, or are they using a common "catalogue of complaints" against Gentiles (as there are similar complaints in other first-century Jewish writings about Gentiles)?

Of these verses, the Romans passage is often cited as a "lynch pin" text because the Apostle Paul seems to make his argument based on the natural order ("natural" vs. "unnatural" passions). But at another place Paul uses nature to justify his position on the proper length of men's and women's hair and the need for women to wear head coverings.[8] As it turns out, arguing

---

[8] I Corinthians 11:2-16

from nature was a common rhetorical device in Paul's day, employed by many contemporaries of the Apostle, and was like saying today, "The conventional wisdom is..."

What are the four basic views of Bible teachings?

Most I have talked to fall into one of four groups regarding these verses, depending on how they address two questions. The first we've named directly at several points already: Do the passages refer to anything like the phenomena of life-long, monogamous or mutually consensual same-gendered relationships that we know of today? (It's worth noting that the word "homosexual" was not present in the ancient world but was add to the English vocabulary in the 19th century.) The second issue we've only alluded to: Whether the passages refer to the phenomenon we are describing today, are we bound to ethical determinations made by persons living in vastly diverse cultures and times and whose understanding of the world and of God's activity was shaped and limited by their own cultural viewpoints.

Depending on how you answer those two critical questions, you will likely fall into one of our groups.

1. The passages in question refer to homosexual practice in all times and cultures and so universally prohibit such practice.
2. The passages do not refer to homosexuality as we know it today and so cannot be prohibiting it. Other passages therefore need to inform our discussions about sexuality in general and homosexual relationships.
3. The passages may or may not refer to homosexuality as we know it, but they — and the larger witness of Scripture — imply a view of nature and creation that supports sexual relationship and union only between man and woman, and so homosexual practice is prohibited.
4. The passages may or may not refer to homosexuality as we know it, but they — and all of Scripture — are conditioned by the cultural and historical realities of the

authors and so offer an incomplete and insufficient understanding of creation and nature and so cannot be used to prohibit homosexual practice today. Rather, one needs to read the larger biblical witness to discern God's hopes for caring, mutually supportive relationships, whether heterosexual or homosexual.

As is often the case, one's larger theological or ideological commitments greatly influence how one reads these seven verses. The first and third positions, for instance, reflect a more conservative view and make it difficult to find anything but condemnation in the Bible for homosexual practice. The second and forth, in contrast, invite a more progressive interpretation of the verses in common and open the way to supporting homosexual relationships as several major mainline church bodies have done.

For those Christians who look to the Bible for moral guidance, two additional questions may be worth considering.

First, do you see yourself represented fairly in one of the four expressions above?

Second, can you imagine that someone holding one of the other three positions is also a faithful Christian who loves God and neighbor and searches the Scripture for guidance in these matters, even if that difference puts you at odds on this matter? How professing Christians answer these questions will greatly determine future discourse on these matters and, more importantly, how they interact with persons who are gay or lesbian.

Sodom and Gomorrah

The following is a commentary by Christina Forrester in the *Huffington Post* on the Sodom and Gomorrah passage from Genesis.

In Ezekiel, it says:[9]

Sodom's sins were pride, gluttony, and laziness, while the poor and needy suffered outside her door. She was proud and committed detestable sins, so I wiped her out, as you have seen.

Most of us, at some point, have heard preachers, right-wing media or leaders talk about the sin of Sodom. Those Sodomites. Sodomization. The abhorrent abomination that was Sodom and Gomorrah! And there was never any question what they were talking about when you heard about Sodom: homosexuals. Perversion. Men having sex with men and lust of the flesh that lead them down a dark path to the point that they wanted to even rape male angels of God! And that was that: God punished Sodom because of the gays. Because sexual perversion had reached such a pinnacle peak that there was not one righteous person left in the city, and God had to burn it. This "fact" has so been embedded, so *sure* in the minds of many conservatives that it has led to entire new theories, doctrines, books and even influenced politics. Here is their reasoning: our society is sinking into the moral sinkhole of the abomination of the gays of Sodom, then fiery judgment will come upon the United States. When we hear the religious right and conservative politicians talk about getting back to "family values" and saving America from the moral corruption overtaking us, they have "Sodom" emblazoned on their metaphorical foreheads.

---

[9] Ezekiel 16:49-50 (NLT)

However, there is just one slight problem with this… the Bible does not say homosexuality was the sin of Sodom. Being gay, as we know it in our culture today, had nothing to do with Sodom and Gomorrah. It is absolutely mind-boggling how so many could completely overlook the point of this often-misquoted Biblical account. One must only *read* Genesis 19 to see this, and then read Ezekiel 16:49-50 for a further interpretation, context and complete understanding that makes the reason for the fire and brimstone crystal clear. But I will start with Genesis.

Violence, sexual violence, mob mentality and other "sins" which are not yet identified have overtaken this city in Genesis 19. The men of the town are so corrupt and violent that they come in a mob to Lot's house demanding to be given the visiting strangers, so they can rape them. Lot, showing the level of acceptance of this culture he has reached and his own desensitization to sin, offers instead his own virgin daughters to the men to rape! The town is so unsafe, so full of violence that there has been a breakdown of order. Chaos, mobs and sexual violence rule. The angels of God practically must drag Lot away, begging him to save his own life and that of his family which says a lot about Lot and has further consequences if you read on. This breakdown of society had nothing to do with homosexuality, but everything to do with moral depravity. The men of the town were motivated by violence, wanting to rape, possibly kill, the visitors. They were ready to beat down the door of their neighbor to do this. This was not monogamous gay marriage, Will and Grace, Elton John's wedding or your friendly lesbian neighbors who are raising their family! It had nothing to do with being gay, and it is not inferred as such in the scripture.

The problem is that people have continued to use this narrative for applause lines, political purposes, or maybe because they were simply under false teaching and genuinely believed it to be true, never actually checking the Bible for themselves. So, one must ask, or should be asking, how *did* the city get to the point where a foreigner cannot visit and walk outside a house without threat of gang rape? What *were* the sins of Sodom that lead to the

Genesis proclamation: "*…we are going to destroy this place. The outcry to the Lord against its people is so great that he has sent us to destroy it*"? It does not tell us in Genesis what this outcry was besides showing us the point to which this city had fallen, but in the book of Ezekiel it explains it quite well.

> *Sodom's sins were pride, gluttony, and laziness, while the poor and needy suffered outside her door. She was proud and committed detestable sins, so I wiped her out, as you have seen.*[10]

Another translation reads:

Now this was the sin of your sister Sodom: She and her daughters were arrogant, overfed and unconcerned; they did not help the poor and needy. They were haughty and did detestable things before me…)[11]"

Proud. Greedy. Unconcerned while the poor and needy were suffering. Arrogance. This was the sin of Sodom. Every time those who were "overfed" and arrogant denied the needs of the poor, the vulnerable in society – that was the outcry against the Lord, clearly.

This understanding of the truth of God's word changes things. When we preach about fire and brimstone, abomination before the Lord and how America is morally and spiritually failing, I will not deny that I believe this may be true, according to the Bible, which says: *They were greedy! Prideful! They had plenty while showing no concern for the poor, the sick, the vulnerable!* Put this into context in today's language and this is what we have: those who have plenty but wish to deny the sick the health care they need. Those who themselves can afford to take care of the health needs of an aging parent or the special needs of a disabled child, but are unconcerned with the plight of those who have no way to pay for

---

[10] Ezekiel 16:49-50
[11] New International Version

such care, to the point that they are willing to move all of heaven and earth to desperately strip away even the hope of the availability of health care for millions. The poorest of the poor in society who rely on Medicaid and food stamps because their jobs don't pay enough to buy both food and rent and health care, or they are disabled and have no options. *This is the abomination spoken of.*

What is the sin of a potential New Sodom? Looking on as people share their stories, one after another, about what will happen to their lives if an already too-expensive health care system is dismantled and defunded, yet callously going about spending their energy on doing just that. Giving gifts in the form of tax breaks to those few who already have plenty, while millions are suffering outside their door. Proud and detestable. And it does not end at health care: homelessness is on the rise, and they want to defund affordable housing initiatives. Extreme poverty and hunger affects millions in the richest country on earth, yet they are against a livable wage and want to cut food stamps. Mentally ill individuals and drug addicts are in prison instead of receiving the care they need, as private prison profits line their donor's pockets. All of this is the epitome of a Biblical definition of Sodom.

Ironically, it is this same group who spends great resources to fight LGBT rights. They protest about where people use the toilet in public restrooms, who can serve in our military and who gets married to whom. If their core reason for doing so has anything to do with what they were taught about the sins of Sodom, may they receive this as a new Sunday school lesson, not from Christina Forrester but straight out of the Word of God, which I believe is *"living and active, sharper than any two-edged sword."*[12]

---

[12] Hebrews 4:12

Reincarnation May Have an Answer

In my book, *Perception*, chapter 23,[13] I make a Biblical case for reincarnation. In the Bible, there are surprising statements that could lead to the conclusion that reincarnation was the accepted view in the time of Jesus and in the early Christian church.

In summary, besides the writings of the church fathers, the John the Baptist-Elijah episode of Matthew 11 and the Jesus-blind man's sin event of John 9 point to an inescapable conclusion about reincarnation and the Bible.

Reincarnation or re-embodiment, later repressed by the church in the Middle Ages, offers some possible answers to the questions about the reason for the diversity of sexual preferences as well as other physical conditions.

Past Life Regression during hypnosis has proven to be a way of discovering how past lifetimes are interconnected to our present life, relationships, situations, goals, pursuits or problems encountered in this lifetime.

So why do we pick one kind of life rather than another and why a homosexual life? I personally do not believe we choose a heterosexual life as opposed to a homosexual life or vice versa without a reason. As spiritual beings, we have a natural compulsion to learn and grow. It's called the will to expand, one of three of our attributes and the attributes of God. Therefore, we have all chosen our present lifetime to be straight, bi, transgender or gay to learn specific lessons and to continue certain growth factors.

At a higher level of consciousness - before we entered this lifetime - we chose to work on certain themes, to overcome given blockages and limitations, to develop certain personal qualities of the soul and to make our unique contribution to the universe. We carefully selected our culture, background, race, sex, parents, childhood experiences and sexual orientation to work on our intended life-themes. These life-themes will, naturally, require

---

[13] Yeaw, James *Perception*. CreateSpace, 2013

personal and spiritual growth: coming to know ourselves, learning to love, realizing our oneness with others, overcoming blockages and limitations, expressing our potential and strengths, transcending the Ego, becoming whole, being creative, being full of joy.

Our life-themes develop personal qualities or strengths. These life-themes are fashioned to learn forgiveness, appreciation of beautiful things, creativity and productivity, courage, leadership, wisdom, or faith. Also, responsibility, compassion, inner peace, intellectual curiously, or a sense of humor or honesty and integrity or the ability to make a commitment. Maybe to consistently stand up for our principles, values and ideals is our life-theme. If so, we create circumstances, which provide us with appropriate challenges in which to develop these.

Michael Millett, a therapist states that his beliefs about homosexuality and past lives are borne out in his work and experience as a therapist and healer since the mid 90`s, has worked with all kinds of people from all over the world. He believes that if a gay life is selected, the soul might have chosen several themes as life focuses within the gay life to learn and grow from as it does with all its choices. Perhaps `honesty` is the life-theme. These manifests through being honest and "coming out" to friends and family, despite fears of rejection.

Perhaps the soul chose `love` as a theme and this specific learning about love and type of love might only be attained by forming a loving and committed relationship with a partner of the same sex. Even choosing `integrity` as the life-theme and achieving this aim by choosing a gay life and then getting involved in a crusade or campaign for gay rights. Maybe the soul of the gay man or woman chose these themes or in part or other life-themes in which their gayness is crucial to their learning and growth.

There are other views or interpretations for homosexuality within a past life context are ones that most therapists may not feel particularly probable with is that confusion can occur when a soul changes over from a life as a member of one gender to that of the other. Souls reincarnate not only into diverse cultures and periods, but also as both men and women, during their many lives. The reincarnating soul could bring with it many of the former characteristics from past personalities and, when these are very strong; they could easily overshadow the new personality. It has been said that gender change may be further complicated if, in the former life, the person had been very active sexually and strongly attached to sexual gratification.

Another thought is that a homosexual incarnation is a `bridge` in a transition from one gender to another. The thinking behind this is that if we have a series of lives as a woman, it is a big switch to go directly to an incarnated life as a man, or vice versa. So, a homosexual or bisexual incarnation is a chance to kind of be `between` for a while, and then once adjusted, incarnate as a different gender than before.

The past never causes what is happening now, or we would be victims. The soul does not have to suffer to progress. Suffering is only good for the soul if it teaches us how not to suffer again. The present moment is always our point of being and power.

The past has impact upon us, but we make the choices, here and now of how to be happy in our life. What is more, the past is not fixed - any more than the future is fixed. We have countless probable pasts and probable futures, all of which already exist - and which constantly shift and change, like a kaleidoscope, according to our beliefs and circumstances right now and the way we handle them. We can and do heal the past, in this and other lifetimes, often without being aware of it but very mindful of it through past life therapy and healing. We can also drop any negative karma - by choosing to learn the lessons, by forgiving ourselves, or by working with our past choices. Everything is flexible; everything can be understood, healed and developed. Everything is open to change.

We are eternal beings, who existed before we were born and will exist after we "die". A synthesis of all that has gone before and our growing and unfolding never ends no matter how we choose to do it. We are here to be free, have choice, develop

and learn to have fun, and consciously create success for
ourselves through many frameworks and life-styles. We must
begin to see that everything and everyone in our life has a greater
significance than we have ever imagined. The fundamental learning
is to forgive and love ourselves and others as we are, whether
- gay, straight, bi-sexual or transgender. And to love ourselves and
others as we were.

We may choose to differ on opinions about
homosexuality, reincarnation or any other concept. It was never
recorded that Jesus spoke of nor was concerned about
homosexuality, but he had a primary concern. It was the core
message of his life. He said,[14]

> *Love the Lord your God with all your heart and with all your
> soul and with all your mind and with all your strength.' The
> second is this: 'Love your neighbor as yourself.' There is no
> commandment greater than these.*

---

[14] Mark 12:30-31

'Nudge from Jesus' changes minister's gay marriage views

By Niraj Warikoo

Ann Arbor, Michigan — When the Rev. Ken Wilson [15]was younger, he didn't know anyone who was openly gay. Like many of his peers, he saw people in the LGBT community as criminals, perverts or homos, a bigoted insult he heard in school.

And when he started his church in the 1970s in Ann Arbor, the evangelical pastor maintained a policy of not allowing gays who were actively sexual.

But about a dozen years ago, the founder and leader of Vineyard Church of Ann Arbor started to have some misgivings about his views. Members of his Christian congregation were coming forward to talk about siblings and children who were openly identified as gay.

In 2011, he said he "got a strong nudge from Jesus," telling him to write a letter to his congregation about his changing views on gay issues, the 62-year-old minister said.

It was a slow process, one that involved prayer, introspection and scholarship as he pored over the Bible and interpretations of it from various writers. Last month, the long letter he wrote to his congregation was published as a book that embraces LGBT people.

Experts say it might be the first time the pastor of a large evangelical Christian congregation in Michigan, and maybe the United States, has come out so openly in favor of gay people and same-sex marriage.

The move comes at a time of intense debate in Michigan over gay marriage after a ruling two weeks ago by a federal judge in Detroit that legalized gay marriage, a ruling currently being appealed.

At least one out of every four Michiganders identify themselves as evangelical or born-again, the biggest religious group in the state, according to studies. For evangelicals — many of whom are conservative and take the Bible's words seriously if not literally — it's a wrenching debate that goes to the core of their beliefs.

"It's about welcoming previously excluded groups," Wilson said of his decision. "That's what it means to be evangelical — to make the good news accessible to those who haven't had access to it. That's my task. That's what a church is supposed to do."

But for many evangelicals, Wilson's views in his book — "*A Letter to my Congregation*:[16] An evangelical pastor's path to embracing people who are gay, lesbian, and transgender into the company of Jesus" — are controversial.

The national leadership of the Vineyard denomination, which has about 1,500 churches, "is not at all supportive of what I'm doing," he said.

And the leadership at many evangelical churches in metro Detroit are still very much opposed to same-sex marriage.

While support for gay marriage may be increasing overall, it's still low for white evangelicals, the group least likely among those surveyed to support it, according to the Pew Research Center. A survey released last month by Pew said 23% of white evangelicals back same-sex marriage, the same amount as last year. In contrast, support for gay marriage has increased among other groups, such as Catholics and mainline Protestants, Pew said.

Wilson's move sparked a backlash within his own congregation, with some people leaving and ending their financial support in the past two years as he became more public about

---

[16] Wilson, Ken *A Letter to My Congregation* Read the Spirit Books, 2016 See also: Hansen, **Adolf,** *Is It Time?: Helping Laity and Clergy Discuss Homosexuality One Question at a Time. From a Catholic perspective: Tedesco, Mark That Undeniable Longing: My Road to and from the Priesthood*

embracing gays. The church's income has dropped 12%, in part because of him coming out in favor of LGBT people.

He faced a similar challenge when he decided in 2004 he would welcome people who accepted scientific theories of human evolution and in 2006, when "I made it clear Christians had an obligation to care for the environment and that climate change was something we had to take seriously."

But his congregation survived both of those moves, and he said it will weather this controversy, too. Decades ago, evangelical churches like Vineyard "had a strict policy against remarriage after divorce," Wilson said, given that Jesus said people should not remarry.

But that changed, and Wilson could not see any reason to also exclude gay people.

Most congregants are supportive of Wilson.

"God is unhappy when we turn anyone away from the church or him," said Penny Johnson, 55, of Livonia. "Being evangelical means that you bring people to Jesus. You don't turn them away."

Johnson said she was raised by a single mom at a time when many evangelical Christians frowned upon people like her and those who were divorced.

"We've overcome that for the most part," and need to do that now with LGBT people, she said.

"I have family, friends who are LGBTQ (lesbian, gay, bisexual, transgender, queer) and the fact that I am a Christian and go to church is, quite frankly, off-putting to people in that community," she said. Gays "are feeling like they're being turned away from the church."

That happened to Lisa Ruby, 49, and her wife, Lisa Carico, 42, a lesbian couple who were looking for a church.

They could have joined a liberal house of worship that welcomed gays, but "we didn't want a crunchy granola church like Unitarians, where they don't talk about God or the Bible," Ruby said. My partner wanted "something very Bible thumping, a lot of Jesus. She liked a lot of church in her church."

Raised Jewish, Ruby felt the same way: "I like a lot of Bible in my religion."

But many evangelical churches were homophobic and didn't accept gays, they said, including Wilson's church at first. Five years ago, when they tried to join, Wilson suggested to the couple that they find a different church. Carico came back later the following year and Ruby then got involved with the church's single women's ministry.

"No one really talked about" the issue of their sexual orientation, Ruby said. "It was like 'don't ask, don't tell.' "

As Wilson started becoming more open to LGBT people, they grew increasingly at home in the church.

"We've lost church members" because of Wilson's changed views, Ruby said. "We've lost money. But he couldn't go forward. It wasn't what he believed anymore."

Wilson's wife, Nancy, also was a pastor. She died suddenly in 2012. She was known for always emphasizing "love, love, love," said Ruby, who worked with Nancy in the women's ministry.

Ken Wilson also stressed love, but he's "very smart, very intellectual," Ruby said.

"He would have to find it in the Bible. He is a scholar. He couldn't just say, 'gay people are great, love them, let them in the church.' He needed to figure it for himself, not just in his heart, but in his head."

Ken Wilson did that, embarking on a spiritual and academic journey that had him trying to understand Bible verses that conservatives say clearly prohibit sexual activity between people of the same gender.

"I take the Bible very seriously," Wilson said. "It's inspired, it's God's word in written form, and I do not dismiss the text and scriptures that speaks this question.

"When the Bible prohibits same-sex sex, what was the historical context for that? There's no real indication monogamous, gay partnerships were the aim of the biblical texts, but there were some very clearly examples of exploitative same-sex sexuality, like temple prostitution or slave sex, masters requiring slaves to perform sexual services as part of their ownership of them.

"In the New Testament, there was pederasty, where older men providing mentoring to underage prepubescent males in exchange for sexual services ... The Sodom and Gomorrah story is about gang rape. It's not about anything like loving monogamous relationships. To apply that to the issue of homosexuality is a gross misuse of scripture."

Some evangelical theologians agree, including James Brownson, a professor of New Testament at Western Theological Seminary in Holland, whose 2013 book *Bible, Gender, Sexuality: Reframing the Church's Debate on Same-Sex Relationships*[17] made the evangelical case for same-sex relationships.

For both straight and gay couples, Wilson preaches that sex should be between two people who are in committed relationships for life.

But the issue for Wilson was not just an abstract theological debate. It involved real people in his congregation, which has about 500-600 in attendance on Sundays.

"I think about this pastorally, not politically," he said. "Pastors have to protect families and couples who are vulnerable from the spotlight and the vitriol of this intense controversy."

Tanya Luhrmann, a professor of anthropology at Stanford, said that Wilson's views will become more common in years to come given increasing acceptance of gays among young people.

"I think this debate is over," Luhrmann said. "There's been such a rapid tipping point towards the tolerance of homosexuality. It's just so clear."

White evangelical Protestant millennials[18] are twice as likely as the oldest generation, aged 68 and older, to support same-sex marriage. This is 43% to 19%, according to a survey released in February by the Public Religion Research Institute.

---

[17] **Brownson, James** *Bible, Gender, Sexuality: Reframing the Church's Debate on Same-Sex Relationships Eerdmans, 2013*
[18] Ages 18-33

Wilson's views seem to have changed hearts inside his congregation. The Monday after same-sex marriage was legalized, he asked the congregation if anyone wanted to help give Communion.

Carico is usually introverted, but volunteered. A woman in the church who was raised conservative went up to Carico to get Communion specifically from her.

She told Carico she had been struggling with Wilson's new views, but now accepted them. The woman then started crying hard.

"It was so incredible," Ruby said, recalling the moment. "It was beautiful."

When Biblical Objections Fail

It is interesting that when the Biblical objections fail, those who oppose inclusion and marriage equality turn to a other reasons as to why homosexuality is wrong. Here are some of those objections that I have heard expressed.

Nature: "It's Not Natural"

The most basic argument presented by same-sex marriage opponents purports that marriage between two people of the same sex is "not natural". At this level of the debate there is very little exploration of the inherent validity of same-sex relationships but rather a fixation on the notion that homosexuality is unnatural: "It's Adam and Eve, not Adam and Steve," the opponents quip.

In reality, marriage is a societal institution. The natural world or "God" didn't create marriage, humans did.

Procreation: "Relationships and Marriage is for Procreation"

With the procreation argument, opponents of equality argue that the institution of marriage is essentially in place to assist with procreation and the raising of children. They reason that because two people of the same sex cannot procreate that they should not be allowed to marry. While children may indeed be a feature of many heterosexual marriages the capacity to procreate does not determine the legal validity of marriages. There are many married couples who cannot biologically have children or who choose not to. The procreation argument ignores the fact that people marry for a wide range of reasons unrelated to procreation including love, friendship and companionship.

Religion: "It's Against My Religion"

And of course, there is religious-based arguments that lead the way in efforts to oppose the legalization of same-sex marriage in America. "Religious beliefs" are regularly made by those who seek to rationalize their support of discrimination via religion. Marriage is a religious institution, they argue, and not one for society to tamper with. Given that the United States is a secular nation, religion should play no role in any discussion about civil and societal laws. In order to legally marry there is absolutely no requirement for a religious ceremony to be held. In this sense, marriage is not a religious institution but a socio-legal one governed by the state. Religious beliefs about marriage should never be enshrined in laws in ways that restrict the freedom of others who do not share those beliefs.

Redefinition: "You're Trying to Redefine the Institution"
Opponents argue that marriage has always been between a man and a woman and that it should stay that way. They say that efforts to legalize same-sex marriage will fundamentally alter the institution for the worse. History reveals, however, that marriage laws in countries across the globe have been *modified repeatedly in response to evolving cultural norms. There* was a time when women were the legal property of their husbands. There was a time when a man and a woman of different races couldn't marry each other. Removing discrimination from the institution of marriage does not redefine "marriage" — it simply makes the institution more accessible and reflects the evolution of society.

Sanctity: "It's a Threat to the Sanctity of Marriage"
With roots in religion, the sanctity argument posits that marriage is a "sacred" institution that only heterosexual couples should have access to. Allowing same-sex couples to marry apparently poses a "threat" to "traditional marriage" as though somehow heterosexual married couples will all be at risk of divorcing when two people of the same sex marry each other. If those who use the "sanctity" argument were genuinely concerned about the institution of marriage they'd focus their efforts on helping those married couples who are at risk of divorcing. If

marriage was so "sacred" they'd also be pursuing the outlawing of divorce.

Children: "It Will Harm the Children"

Opponents of equality frequently make use of flawed research studies to insinuate that allowing same-sex couples to marry will harm children. They argue that children need a "mom and a dad" in order to flourish in life and that legalizing same-sex marriage denies children this opportunity of "normalcy." Multiple studies across the social sciences have repeatedly demonstrated that there is no difference in psychosocial outcomes between children raised by opposite-sex couples and those raised by same-sex couples. There is no evidence that children are psychologically harmed by having two dads or two moms. The American Psychological Association, the American Sociological Association, and the American Academy of Pediatrics has each endorsed the legalization of same-sex marriage and its capacity to provide a stable familial framework for children.

Reverse Discrimination: "Religious People Will Be Discriminated Against"

Some opponents of marriage equality describe a future in which religious people become the new "victims" of oppression. They talk of charity-based religious organizations being "forced out of business" for "sticking to their beliefs" about marriage. In this reverse scenario, gay people are apparently "hateful" for wanting to be treated equally in society. In no case is a church legally required to perform same-sex marriage ceremonies. Religious groups and churches are still free to pick and choose who they will and won't marry. Organizations that receive public money, however, and which must adhere to anti-discrimination laws, should rightly be challenged if they engage in discrimination against a protected class of people.

Slippery Slope: "It Will Lead to Marriage Involving Animals, Siblings, Children, or Groups of People!"

Slippery slope arguments suggest that legalizing gay marriage will serve as a "gateway" for the legalization of marriage involving animals, siblings, children, or groups of people. People who present these scenarios portray a catastrophic future with society crumbling under the weight of rampant immorality and social discord. Efforts to legalize same-sex marriage, however, simply aim to provide same-sex couples with equal access to marriage laws — there is no intention to change the fundamental definition of marriage as the legal union between two adult human beings who have no direct biological connection with each other. Facts are useful in this regard: of the many countries that have legalized same-sex marriage, none of them has subsequently considered or legalized marriage involving animals, children, siblings, or groups of people.

Civil Unions: "Civil Unions Are Enough"

Some opponents of same-sex marriage support the creation of a "separate but equal" platform in which straight couples and gay couples receive the same relationship rights and benefits, but from within different institutional frameworks. They argue that "marriage" should be left exclusively for opposite-sex couples and that same-sex couples should be granted "civil unions."

History has demonstrated that this "separate but equal" approach doesn't work. Various countries which initially permitted "civil unions" for same-sex couples have subsequently enacted marriage equality legislation. These jurisdictions have pursued such changes because civil union legislation, no matter how valiant the effort, is not able to provide the same rights and benefits as legal marriage. Having a two-class system continues to maintain the erroneous notion that one group is more superior to another group.

States' Rights: "States Have the Right to Oppose It"

This position stresses that states have a constitutional right to make their own decisions about the legalization of same-sex marriage which may include banning it. Ironically, most advocates of this argument also support the Defense of Marriage Act, a law which allows the federal government to deny more than one thousand federal rights and benefits to same-sex couples legally married at the state level. The maintenance of a system which allows some states to recognize same-sex marriage and others not to, and which allows the federal government to ignore legal same-sex marriages performed at the state level, sets up a cumbersome and extremely complicated national map of unequal rights.

Testimonies

These popular Christian writers, pastors or musicians, in no order, are some of many that have publicly broken from the traditional hardline position against same-sex marriage.

Jen Hatmaker

Evangelical leader, author and HGTV star Jen Hatmaker publicly changed her views on gay marriage in 2016. Both a Facebook post calling for LGBT acceptance and comments about supporting same-sex marriage in an interview with RNS led LifeWay Christian Stores to quit selling her books in October.

Jim Wallis

The founder of *Sojourners* magazine, Jim Wallis was raised evangelical. He defended traditional marriage in a 2008 *Christianity Today* article, saying he wasn't sure he'd perform a same-sex blessing, although he did express support for gay and lesbian civil rights. In 2013, Wallis answered "yes" when asked if he supported same-sex marriage in a *Huffington Post* interview.

Matthew Vines

After taking a leave of absence from Harvard University to study the Bible and homosexuality, Matthew Vines gave a speech at his church about accepting gay Christians that has amassed over 1 million views on YouTube since 2012. He also started The Reformation Project, a nonprofit trying to "reform church teaching on sexual orientation and gender identity," and wrote the book "*God and the Gay Christian: The Biblical Case in Support of Same-Sex Relationships.*"[19]

Rob Bell

The former pastor of Mars Hill Bible Church publicly stated his views on gay marriage while speaking at San Francisco's Grace Cathedral in 2013. He then reaffirmed them during an Odyssey Networks interview the same week. At Grace Cathedral, he also said evangelicals should no longer be assumed to be conservatives. He described "a

---

[19] Vines, Matthew *God and the Gay Christian: The Biblical Case in Support of Same-Sex Relationships* Convergent Books, 2015

very narrow, politically intertwined, culturally ghettoized, evangelical subculture" that he sees dying out.

Trey Pearson

In a post on his website titled "My Coming Out Letter," Christian rock musician Trey Pearson told fans that he identified as a gay man, despite being married with children. As he explains in the letter, published in June 2016, he was raised in a faith that taught him "sexual orientation was a matter of choice," so he repressed his sexual desires most of his life. Since coming out, he has written about life as a gay Christian and created a music video depicting his experience.

Julie Rodgers

Although she has identified as gay since high school, Julie Rodgers has officially supported gay marriage for only a few years. As she has chronicled on her blog and in *The Washington Post,* she first spent a long time advocating celibacy for Christians who were gay or lesbian. Now, she speaks and writes as an advocate for LGBT Christians.

Rachel Held Evans

In 2015, *The Washington Post* called Christian author Rachel Held Evans "the most polarizing woman in evangelicalism." This label comes from her positions on LGBT rights and homosexuality, topics she's grappled with publicly since starting her blog in 2008. In one of her old posts, "An Evangelical's Response to Homosexuality," she refuses to choose a side of the issue but does admit to wondering if the evangelical church "has it wrong." In more recent years, she has referred to herself as an "ally" and wrote about LGBT Christians in her 2015 book *Searching for Sunday.*[20]

Joel Hunter

The 2016 Pulse nightclub shooting caused Pastor Joel Hunter to re-evaluate his views on LGBT issues. While he said recently that his church, Northland, A Church Distributed, will maintain that the Bible prohibits gay relationships, he now believes conservative churches should welcome and support those of all sexual orientations. In May, Northland hosted a public forum to discuss LGBT issues within the church.

---

[20] Evans, Rachel Held *Searching for Sunday: Loving, Leaving and Finding the Church* Thomas Nelson, 2015

Vicky Beeching

Christian rock star Vicky Beeching still considered herself an evangelical, even after coming out via an interview with The Independent in 2014. During her keynote address at the 2015 Gay Christian Network's annual conference, the U.K.-based singer said she still loves the church. According to her official site, she now works as a speaker and writer, often discussing her personal journey and LGBT issues in the church.

10101 West Coggins Drive
Sun City Arizona 85351
623-974-6443

See us on the web at:
www.unitysc.org